Outcomes and Effectiveness of Family Support Services

a research review

June Statham

INSTITUTE OF
EDUCATION
UNIVERSITY OF LONDON   in association with Thomas Coram Research Unit

First published in 2000 by the Institute of Education, University of London,
20 Bedford Way, London WC1H 0AL

Pursuing Excellence in Education

British Library Cataloguing in Publication Data:
A catalogue record for this publication is available from the British Library

ISBN 0 85473 627 1

Design by Tim McPhee
Page make-up by Cambridge Photosetting Services

Production services by
Book Production Consultants plc, Cambridge

Printed by Watkiss Studios Ltd, Biggleswade, Beds

Contents

Acknowledgements

This publication was prepared as part of a research study entitled 'Supporting families: a comparison of outcomes and economic evaluation of services for children in need in two areas', which was funded by the Wales Office for Research and Development. I should like to thank my co-workers on the project, Sally Holtermann and Gill Winter, for their hard work and enthusiasm. The support and encouragement of Ann Mooney, Peter Moss and Peter Aggleton at the Thomas Coram Research Unit was much appreciated. I am also grateful for the moral and financial support of Gerry Evans and Marcus Hill at WORD.

The views expressed in this publication are those of the author and do not necessarily represent the views of the Wales Office for Research and Development, the Thomas Coram Research Unit or the Institute of Education, University of London.

Dr June Statham, May 2000

Introduction

Current government policy stresses the importance of evaluation and assessing the outcomes of services that are provided or purchased by local authorities. There is a new emphasis on evidence-based practice, grounded in information from research that attempts to show what works both in individual cases and in the planning of services. Agencies in both the statutory and independent sectors are increasingly expected to demonstrate successful outcomes in order to obtain funding and meet government targets. There have been a number of well-argued criticisms of this approach, especially its application to the social welfare field (e.g. Parton, 1999), but the reality is that many practitioners and planners are currently facing unprecedented demands to monitor and evaluate their work.

This paper[1] reviews the evidence for the effectiveness of different kinds of family support services, focusing on those that social services departments are likely to commission or provide to support families who are disadvantaged or experiencing particular difficulties in their lives. Whilst universal services such as those provided by health, education, leisure and libraries are an important component of any family support strategy, they are outside the remit of this paper. It also describes some of the published tests and scales that have been used in research studies to measure outcomes for children and families who have received such support. The aims of the paper are:

- to describe different methods of evaluation, and outline some of the problems and issues raised by evaluating social welfare provision in general and family support services in particular
- to provide a brief overview of the research evidence on 'what works' in different kinds of family support provided for children in need
- to bring together information on various measures and scales which have been used to evaluate family support services.

The rest of the paper is divided into three parts, addressing each of these aims. It begins with a discussion of what is meant by the term 'family support'.

Note

1. This paper has been prepared as part of a research project commissioned by the Wales Office of Research and Development. The project is comparing outcomes and costs of family support services for children in need in two local authorities in North Wales, and is due to be completed in December 2000.

1 *The conceptual framework*

WHAT DO WE MEAN BY FAMILY SUPPORT SERVICES? Despite the current emphasis on the importance of family support, there is a great deal of confusion about what the term actually means and the services it covers. It is often thought of as the opposite end of the spectrum from child protection, and equated with promotional/ preventive services which are offered to families before their difficulties become too severe. In the USA, a clear distinction is made between the terms 'family support' and 'family preservation':

> *Family support services are intended for families who are coping with the normal stresses of parenting, to provide reassurance, strengthen a family facing child-rearing problems, or prevent the occurrence of child maltreatment. By contrast, family preservation services are designed to help families at serious risk or in crisis, and are typically available only to families whose problems have brought them to the attention of child protective services, the juvenile justice system, or the mental health system.* (McCroskey and Meezan, 1998)

But in fact services to support families can be provided at any of the levels of intervention that have been identified by Pauline Hardiker and colleagues in their grid framework for mapping and planning services (Hardiker, Exton and Barker, 1995). In Hardiker's model, after a 'base' level of universal services available to all families, there are four levels of intervention. The first comprises services offered to vulnerable groups and communities, the second is services for families suffering early stresses and temporary crises, the third offers support to those experiencing severe stresses and at risk of family breakdown, and the fourth describes services offered once children have been removed from home. Although family support is often identified with levels 1 and 2, and it is certainly the case that many services will aim to support parents to bring up their children within their own home, family support may also encompass the preservation of connections between families and children looked after.

Definitions of family support in the literature provide another indication of what the term is thought to cover. The Audit Commission defines family support as: 'Any activity or facility provided either by statutory agencies or by community groups or individuals, aimed at providing advice and support to parents to help them in bringing up their children' (Audit Commission, 1994).

Various researchers have provided similar definitions:

> *The type of services which local authorities have a duty to provide or purchase for the purpose of promoting the welfare of children in need, wherever possible within their own homes.* (Gibbons, 1992)

Family support is about the creation and enhancement, with and for families in need, of locally based (or accessible) activities, facilities and networks, the use of which have outcomes such as alleviated stress, increased self esteem, promoted parental/carer/ family competence and behaviour and increased parental/carer capacity to nurture and protect children. (Hearn, 1995)

As well as the type of service, a key element of these definitions is the way in which services are provided, which emphasizes enabling families to use resources as and when they need them and to use their own skills to assist each other. In fact one study of family support, in Northern Ireland, concluded that family support is better viewed as 'a policy direction and style of working', rather than as a collection of particular services (Higgins, Pinkerton and Devine, 1997).

WHAT DO WE MEAN BY EVALUATION?

A second question is what is meant by evaluation. A distinction is commonly made between different types of evaluation:

- *process* evaluation, which looks at the way a service is delivered – for example, how it was set up, how its principles are translated into practice
- *output* evaluation, which measures the 'products' of a service – for example, how many families were served, how many practitioners were trained
- *outcome* evaluation, which assesses the impact of the service on those who receive it, or on society more generally; both short- and longer-term effects can be measured.

The terms, in particular the distinction between outputs and outcomes, are not used consistently. For example, Cheetham et al. (1997) talk of service-based and client-based outcomes (the nature, extent and quality of what is provided versus the effects of a provision on its recipients). Knapp (1984) refers to intermediate and final outcomes (indicators of performance, service or activity versus indicators of effect, influence or impact).

Strictly speaking, effectiveness studies involve being able to make claims about the *causes* of various outcomes, and so require a careful research design that will enable any change to be attributed to a particular intervention. But information about process (the way a service is delivered) is also essential for understanding how an intervention works, and hence how it might be replicated. On the basis of a number of studies in the USA, Dunst, Trivette and Deal (1994) conclude that many elements of effective services centre around interpersonal aspects of the relationship between service providers and families, and that 'it matters as much *how* professionals assist families in mobilising resources as it does *which* sources are mobilised'. There are many valuable studies, in the UK as well as the USA, that are concerned solely with this aspect of evaluation. However, studies of the effectiveness of family support services also require information about the impact of services on children and families.

HOW IS EFFECTIVENESS ASSESSED?

The main research designs used to evaluate interventions are the randomized controlled trial (RCT); the before-and-after study either with or without a control group (these are also known as pre-test/post-test studies); longitudinal or cohort studies; and a large body of work that can best be described as descriptive. Experimental designs (such as RCTs) and quasi-experimental designs have not been widely used in the social welfare field, and some of the possible reasons for this are discussed below. A useful overview of the different research methods, with examples of particular studies which have used them, can be found in Newman and Roberts (1999).

Randomized controlled trial (RCT)

The randomized controlled trial is a study where one group (the experimental or intervention group) receives a particular service or treatment and another group (the control group) receives a different intervention or none at all. The key aspect of RCTs is that those participating in the study must have an equal chance of being in either group (i.e. they are randomly allocated) so that, with a large enough sample, any factors that might affect the outcome, apart from receiving the service, will be evenly distributed between the two groups and hence balance each other out. The RCT thus has the greatest 'attributive confidence'; in other words, it is the best design for being able to say that it was the service provided that caused any differences in outcome. But it is not always practically feasible or ethically acceptable to allocate families to services randomly, and experimental designs like the RCT have been relatively little used in the social welfare as opposed to the health services field. More common are quasi-experimental or non-experimental designs like those described below.

Before-and-after studies with control group

This is a similar design to the RCT, apart from the fact that allocation to experimental and control group is not random. One group receives a service and another a different service or none at all, and both groups are tested before any service starts and at a similar point some time later. However, the comparison group is chosen from a similar population, such as those on a waiting list for the service or living in a similar neighbourhood. This method depends on the two groups being well matched on any characteristics that may affect outcomes, such as socio-economic status, severity of the problem or the child's age. The problem is knowing in advance which characteristics are relevant and hence need to be controlled for.

Before-and-after studies with no control group

These studies compare measures taken before and after an intervention, but for those using the service only. Although they can demonstrate changes, it is difficult without a control or comparison group to argue that these changes might not have happened anyway over time. However, if a number of before-and-after studies in a given area show similar findings, their 'attributive confidence' is strengthened.

Cohort studies

Cohort studies interview or survey the same group of people at different points in time, often over many years. They can help to identify factors that seem to be associated with particular outcomes – for example, the characteristics of children from poor backgrounds who nevertheless do well later in life. Well-known examples are the National Child Development Study and the National Survey of Health and Development. Such studies can provide a wealth of information on how children develop over time, and can estimate the effects of receiving particular services (for instance, comparing outcomes for children who attended pre-school services with those who did not). However, it is difficult to control statistically for all the other influences on outcomes, and cohort studies do not have the explanatory power of studies that take measures before and after a particular intervention.

Descriptive studies

There are many studies in the social welfare field that fall into this category, including opinion surveys, descriptions of how services are set up and delivered, characteristics of service users and analyses of how far services are accessible and meet families' needs. These provide useful information for planning and improving services, but on their own are insufficient for assessing effectiveness.

ISSUES IN EVALUATING FAMILY SUPPORT SERVICES

The assessment of family support services raises a number of particular difficulties and issues. These have been well summarized in a paper prepared for a cross-departmental government review of provision for young children (Oliver, Smith and Barker, 1997). They include the fact that:

- very few such interventions have been rigorously evaluated
- some evaluations fail to record unanticipated outcomes
- few evaluations are both longitudinal *and* scientifically rigorous
- some outcomes are difficult to measure
- information on processes can be as important as the measurement of outcomes
- evaluations need to take different perspectives and values into account
- small-scale, innovative projects rarely have the funds to evaluate their work.

There is also a broader issue to consider, which is that almost all the evaluative studies have been carried out in countries such as the USA which have a particular approach to the relationship between the state and the welfare of families. Support is provided to individuals who are seen to be struggling or failing; rather than the alternative approach adopted by countries such as Sweden, France and Denmark, which is to provide a relatively high level of support to all families.

In the USA (and the UK), family support policies and practices tend to be focused on poor families, and the great majority of 'children in need' suffer from poverty (Department of Health, forthcoming). Many of the problems that bring them to the attention of social services departments are related to insufficient income. Various commentators have argued for a return to a 'community development' approach to social work (e.g. Cannan and Warren, 1997; Jack, 1997; Smith, 1999) and for an increase in public expenditure on children and young people (Holtermann, 1995). Both the USA and the UK have high levels of child poverty, and the latest evidence on the impact of current government policies to address this suggests that, although child poverty will be reduced, this will be by around one quarter, still leaving some two million children living below the poverty line (Piachaud and Sutherland, 2000). Yet most evaluations of family support have been undertaken within the context of individualistic, as opposed to redistributional or other, types of policies.

Even within the individualistic approach to family support, evaluation poses particular problems.

Finding appropriate outcome measures

Many of the desired outcomes of family support services involve changes in perceptions and attitude, which are generally measured by respondents rating themselves on various scales. A number of scales have been developed covering various aspects of family functioning, well-being and child development (some of these are listed in Table 1, page 14). However, scale scores may be insufficiently sensitive to reveal the complexity of behaviour and attitudes within families. Parker (1991) has warned that 'there is a danger that measuring instruments which seek to reduce complicated phenomena to statistical form will acquire an appearance of objectivity and certainty which is in fact spurious'. Others have noted that 'many evaluations emphasise child development outcomes, which can be measured with some confidence, even though most services are aimed at adult family members' (McCroskey and Meezan, 1998).

Combination of services

Family support services often involve a package of different kinds of support, such as day care for children, counselling for a parent, financial assistance and welfare benefits advice. If a positive outcome is found, it is difficult to know which element of the package is effective.

Timescale over which effects may appear   The length of time between the intervention and the point at which outcomes are assessed may not be long enough to demonstrate any real impact. The demands of funders or government bodies may mean that outcomes have to be assessed before a service has had a chance to have a measurable effect.

Small samples   Specialist family support services that are available on a referral basis may be used by only a small number of families over the period of an evaluation, making it difficult to achieve a large enough sample size to demonstrate significant results.

Outcomes for whom?   Many different parties are involved in family support services – parents, children, service providers, researchers, local and central government – and they may disagree about the objectives of a service and the outcomes that should be measured. Parents may have different views from professionals, or indeed from their children – for example, about whether a child remaining in the family home constitutes a positive outcome or not.

Complexity of family life   In the real world there are many influences on families' lives that may be difficult to monitor and measure. External events such as a bereavement or illness, or a partner leaving or joining the household, are likely to have as much of an impact on the situation as any support services provided by external agencies. In addition, the progress of children and families who have major difficulties may be complex, with improvements and setbacks, depending on which aspects of development are considered and when they are measured (Hill et al., 1995).

The evaluation of social interventions presents problems not generally encountered in more clinical settings. It is interesting that in an analysis of the effectiveness of child and adolescent mental health services, Weisz and colleagues (1995) found that, although studies undertaken in controlled experimental conditions often demonstrated a positive outcome, those undertaken in 'real life' settings of schools or clinics not infrequently produced much more ambiguous results.

THE DEBATE OVER METHODS

There is an ongoing debate between those who acknowledge the difficulties and 'messiness' of evaluating effectiveness in child welfare services, but argue that without a randomly allocated control group and a reasonable sample size it is impossible to say whether it is a particular intervention that is causing an effect (for example, Macdonald, 1996; Oakley, 1996); and those who query the appropriateness of a controlled experimental design in the social welfare field (for example, Trinder, 1996; Parton, 1999). Perhaps the most fruitful approach is to acknowledge that a variety of methods are needed to provide evidence of effectiveness at different levels (Stevens, 1999; Williams, Popay and Oakley, 1999; Guralnick, 1997).

Information on process factors, the 'how' and 'why' an intervention works, is also crucial. However, this review has a particular focus. It is based on studies which include information on *outcomes* as well as process, and which use at least some aspects of an experimental design – such as a control group or a before-and-after comparison. It is not restricted solely to studies using RCTs, nor does it attempt to provide a systematic review along the lines of those often carried out in the health care field, where results of individual controlled trials are amalgamated. The aim of the report is to provide a short, accessible overview of relevant evidence-based research on the effectiveness of family support services for children in need, which will provide a starting point for those wanting to follow up particular topics in more detail.

② *Evidence for effectiveness*

This section of the report briefly reviews what is known about the effectiveness of different kinds of services to support families, covering:

- day care and early education
- family centres
- parenting education
- pre- and post-natal home visiting
- befriending and social support
- interventions to address children's mental health
- services for disabled children and their families
- short-term fostering
- social work support
- family group conferences.

It draws as far as possible on secondary sources of evidence such as existing reviews, in particular the excellent Barnado's 'What works?' series. Individual studies are also described where they are particularly relevant or where they deal with an area not otherwise covered.

DAY CARE AND EARLY EDUCATION

There is an extensive literature on the effects of day care and early education on the cognitive and emotional development of children in general (a useful review is given in Mooney and Munton, 1997). Very few of these studies have used an RCT design. A systematic review by Zoritch and Roberts (1997) found only eight RCT studies out of over 900 identified, all American. They included the well-known Head Start and Perry Pre-school/High Scope projects (McKey et al., 1985; Schweinhart et al., 1993), both of which were targeted on disadvantaged children and looked at effects over a long time period. The evidence from these studies is that day care and early intervention programmes have a positive effect on children's development and success in later life, provided they are of good quality and have appropriate educational components. The effects are strongest where educational programmes for children are combined with support for parents, such as home visits.

Because most studies have been undertaken in the United States, the results cannot automatically be assumed to apply to the UK, nor to children in general rather than those in disadvantaged families on whom the programmes are usually targeted. Two studies currently being undertaken in England should help to remedy this. One is a prospective longitudinal study examining the characteristics of key types of child care and their short- and longer-term effect on children's development from birth to age five. The study is being carried out in Oxford and London, and involves over 700 children (Leach and Barnes, 2000). The second is the Effective Provision of Preschool Education (EPPE) Project, commissioned by the Department for Education and Employment, which is comparing the effectiveness of different types of pre-school provision on children's later attainment at school (Sylva et al., 1999).

Social workers have tended to refer children for day care primarily as a means of reducing stress on parents rather than to focus on children's cognitive development. Day care is provided either in local authority day nurseries or family centres, or through purchasing places in the independent sector (private day nurseries, childminders and playgroups). There is little research evidence on the outcomes for children or families of attending local authority day care centres, although the EPPE project includes 24 such centres in its sample. Outcome data are not yet available, but the first phase of the study showed that on measures of the quality of provision, the local authority centres scored in the 'adequate' to 'good' range; better than playgroups and private day nurseries but worse than LEA nursery schools, classes and combined centres.

Sponsored day care, where the local authority places and pays for children in independent day care services, provides nearly as many places for 'children in need' in England as do local authority nurseries, and more places than the statutory sector in Wales (Cameron and Statham, 1997). Again, little is known about the effectiveness of sponsored day care. A study by Jane Gibbons of family support services in two local areas found that day care was the one service that showed a significant relationship with improved family functioning, especially for lone parents. Practical help for parents in the form of fees for playgroup attendance appeared to have more effect on parent–child outcomes than help in the form of small amounts of financial assistance. Gibbons suggests that 'this type of family support perhaps leads to greater resilience and ability to resolve problems, and links isolated parents to other sources of support in local communities' (Gibbons, 1990, p. 225).

An ongoing study for the Department of Health of the use of sponsored day care for children in need (Statham, Dillon and Moss, 2000) is mostly concerned with mapping the extent of provision and the process of placing children, rather than with studying outcomes. However, the final phase of the research is tracking the progress of a small number of families whose children were referred to two sponsored childminding schemes. Preliminary results suggest that while families generally appreciated the service and found it helpful, they often still had a high level of need when the placement ended. There was also a relatively high non-take-up of childminding places, because some parents were ambivalent about using this type of childcare and saw it as a criticism of their parenting abilities.

Early Years Excellence Centres (EECs) were introduced in England as part of the government's National Childcare Strategy, with the aim of developing high quality, integrated early years' services for young children and families that combine education, care and family support. A preliminary evaluation has been carried out of eight of the pilot EECs (Bertram and Pascal, 2000). It concludes that the centres have had a positive impact on children, families, communities and practitioners; for instance, by enhancing children's social, intellectual and physical development and improving the mental and physical health of parents. However, although the case studies and quotes from parents show clearly that the centres provide a valuable and much appreciated service, this preliminary evaluation did not include any before-and-after measures or comparison with parents not using an EEC, so it is difficult to claim that it provides hard evidence of the centres' effectiveness. A longer-term national evaluation of the EEC programme is planned, and four of these centres are also included in the EPPE project described above.

PARENTING EDUCATION

The term 'parenting education'[1] covers a wide variety of activities, methods and client groups. It can be offered on an individual or group basis, in clinics or community settings such as schools and family centres, and as one strand of other family support services. Some programmes aim to help all families learn more about how to bring up their children; others are targeted at families whose children are exhibiting behaviour problems; and still others provide support and education to referred families where there is a risk of family breakdown. Examples of the former include PIPPIN (Parents in Partnership

– Parent Infant Network), PEEP (Peers Early Education Partnership), PAFT (Parents as First Teachers) and the Healthy Child materials (Children in Wales, 1998). Programmes available in the UK to support parents experiencing difficulties include the Parent and Children videotape materials developed by Webster-Stratton and, at the intensive end, Mellow Parenting is a programme designed to support families whose relationship with their children is under severe stress. More information about these programmes and where to obtain them is included in the guide to evidence-based practice published by the Sure Start Unit (1999).

Most research into the effectiveness of parent education has been carried out in the USA, although even there few studies meet the 'gold standard' of the RCT. Barlow (1997) identified 255 studies of group-based parenting programmes which aimed to improve the behaviour of children aged 3 to 10, but only 18 of these met her criteria for providing evidence of effectiveness. Some of the best-designed studies were those by Webster-Stratton, Kolpacoff and Hollingsworth (1988) and Cunningham, Bremner and Boyle (1995). In the UK, Smith (1997) found 15 evaluations of parenting programmes, including those aimed at all parents as well as parents experiencing difficulties with their children. However, most did not have a control group or compare before-and-after measures. Two exceptions were those by Lawes (1992) and Sutton (1992). Smith concludes that 'we still do not know enough about the effectiveness of parenting programmes, despite the wealth of anecdotal evidence and the practically universal praise from the parents who do participate in these programmes'.

An important study completed since Smith's review is an evaluation of the Mellow Parenting programme, funded by the Department of Health (Puckering et al., 1999). This is an intensive group programme for families with fairly severe parenting difficulties including child protection issues. The study compared 54 mothers attending the Mellow Parenting programme at three family centres and a community centre in Scotland, with a control group of 28 mothers attending another Scottish family centre who were able to use the usual childcare, family counselling and support services. Measures were taken before and after the 14-week course, including videotaped observation of the mother and child during lunchtimes at home. Compared to the control group, the Mellow Parenting group showed significant improvements in the mother's mental state, the child's behaviour and observed mother–child interaction.

Not all mothers benefited from the programme, and a key factor appeared to be their willingness to invest emotional energy in the group and the child. At the follow-up a year later, the mothers who had benefited from the Mellow Parenting groups were significantly more likely than the controls to have maintained that improvement – but not where their partners had been hostile to their involvement in the group, suggesting the importance of involving fathers as well as mothers in parenting programmes. Some family centres are now running couples' or fathers' groups based on the original Mellow Parenting programme.

A number of other evaluations of the effectiveness of parenting programmes are currently being undertaken in the UK. For example, SPOKES (Supporting Parents on Kids Education) is a three-year research project funded by the Department of Health which uses an RCT design to compare different interventions for parents of five-year-old children at risk of behaviour problems. One group attend a school-based programme of parent education based on the Webster-Stratton materials, which lasts for three terms and includes an additional element focused on helping parents to develop their children's literacy skills. A second group is assisted through a helpline to access standard local services (Laurent, 2000).

On the basis of the evidence available by the late 1990s from the USA and elsewhere, most of which has involved work with parents whose children have behaviour problems, Lloyd (1999) has drawn a number of conclusions. There is evidence to show that parent education programmes can improve children's behaviour and that the effects last over time, although a third and sometimes as many as a half of parents continue to experience difficulties. Overall, behaviourally oriented programmes (where parents are trained to use praise and reinforcement effectively) seem to have more impact on children's behaviour than those which emphasize relationships and communication, although the latter have positive outcomes for parents. Group-based parent education programmes are more successful in improving the behaviour of children than working with parents on an individual basis, and are likely to be more cost effective as well as more acceptable to many parents. The way in which parenting programmes are run or facilitated is important, and the most effective approach seems to be an interactive model of learning that values parents' own ideas and experience (see also Roberts and Statham, 1999). Working with parents alone is not enough to achieve long-term change in children, and parenting programmes that include direct work with the child are likely to be more effective than those that do not.

FAMILY CENTRES

There is little rigorous research on the effectiveness of family centres, although there are many useful studies that describe who uses the centres, the types of support that are offered, and how families and referrers think the centres have helped (Statham, 1994; Smith, 1996; Lloyd, 1997). There is also research evaluating the effectiveness of specific services provided within family centres, such as parenting groups (described above), but not the impact of the centres as a whole. One problem for evaluation is the wide range of services that the typical family centre offers; another is the difficulty of defining the target population who use the service.

The descriptive studies provide some interesting information. For example, a study of six Children's Society family centres found that, in areas of high need, there was little difference between the characteristics of those using centres operating on a referred and an open-access basis, suggesting that the latter might be a better way to reach more families in need (Smith, 1996). Another study suggested that although open-access family centres were providing a much valued service, their users were predominantly isolated women in their 20s who used the centres for social support. To benefit a wider range of disadvantaged families, these researchers argued that some centres should adopt more of a community development role, including employing local people (Pithouse and Holland, 1999). A recently completed study into how family centres are working with fathers also concluded that they are used predominantly by women, and perceived as 'highly feminised environments' (Ghate et al., 2000).

There is hardly any research that attempts to measure effectiveness by comparing outcomes for families who attend family centres, especially those operating on an open-access model, with those who do not. A recent study by Davey, Holland and Pithouse (1999) tracked the progress of 41 families who attended a referral-only family centre for up to two years after the initial referral. Much of the data was qualitative, but information was also collected on child protection registrations, legal orders and incidence of re-abuse. There was an increase in the number of children subject to legal orders over this period, probably due to the fact that many referrals were made when care proceedings were beginning. However, numbers on child protection registers decreased markedly during and after attendance at the family centre, and, where information was available, the data suggested a re-abuse level of between 7 and 10 per cent. Although the study did not have a control group, higher re-abuse rates of around 30 per cent have been reported in other UK research (Department of Health, 1995).

One study that did include a comparison group was carried out in South Wales (Pithouse and Lindsell, 1996). Outcomes for families referred to a specialist family centre because of child protection concerns were compared with outcomes for families in similar circumstances in a neighbouring area who were supported only by the local social work team. Although the numbers were small (ten in each group), the outcomes were notably better for those attending the family centre. After a year, none of the families referred to the family centre group had children on the child protection register, in voluntary care or subject to a care order; while the field social worker group had increased numbers of care orders and care proceedings.

PRE- AND POST-NATAL HOME VISITING

This category includes a variety of services such as targeted pre-natal support and additional home visits in the first year or so after birth, by health visitors or 'community mothers'. Most of the experimental studies of the effects of early home visiting have been carried out in the United States, and some have included a long-term follow-up (e.g. Olds et al., 1997). A review by Ian Roberts of over thirty RCTs concluded that 'family support provided by home visitors reduces the incidence of childhood injury, improves maternal well-being, and has positive effects on the parent–child relationship' (Roberts, 1996, p. 222).

It is risky to generalize from research carried out mostly in the USA, but there are a number of studies in the UK that have found similar positive effects. For example, a study of social support in pregnancy (Oakley, Rajan and Grant, 1990) compared outcomes for over 200 women with a history of low birth weight babies who received regular support visits from specially trained midwives during their pregnancy, with a control group of women who received routine ante-natal care. The mothers receiving the support visits were less likely to be admitted to hospital antenatally, to have non-spontaneous deliveries or to suffer from depression and poor health after the birth. Their babies were healthier and their partners more likely to be helpful with their other children. These positive effects were still present a year later, and at the age of seven there were fewer behavioural problems among the children and less anxiety among the mothers in the intervention group (Oakley et al., 1996).

Effective support may be provided by community volunteers as well as by professionals such as health visitors and midwives. The Community Mothers programme in the Republic of Ireland recruited and trained experienced local mothers to visit other mothers with new-born babies. The researchers found that at a year old the children of visited mothers were more likely than the children of those receiving conventional post-natal care to have received all their immunizations, to have been breast fed in their first six months and to be read to by their parents on a daily basis. Their mothers were also less likely to report feeling tired and miserable (Johnson and Molloy, 1995).

BEFRIENDING AND SUPPORT

The best-known home visiting service in the UK for parents of young children (under five) is Home-Start. The scheme operates in most parts of the UK, and involves trained volunteers providing support to families who are experiencing difficulties. There have been several research studies of people receiving help through Home-Start (Van der Eyken, 1982; Shinman, 1994; Oakley et al., 1996; Frost et al., 1996), which report that many users are satisfied with the service and feel that it has helped. However, these generally rely on descriptive measures and none has had a comparison group. The study by Frost and colleagues used a before-and-after design to assess the effectiveness of a three-year Home-Start project funded by the Department of Health in northern England. Forty-six families were interviewed when they first received Home-Start visits and again after six months. Two out of three mothers reported improvements in their well-being, and, among those who were experiencing parenting difficulties, one in three said involvement in Home-Start had helped them make positive and consistent changes. This study intended to establish a control group, but was unable to do so (Frost et al., 1996).

At Queen's University in Belfast, McAuley has been working with professionals and families using the Home-Start service to identify a range of appropriate outcome measures (McAuley, 1999). She is now embarking on an evaluation of the effectiveness of Home-Start schemes in England and Northern Ireland using psychometric tests such as the Parenting Stress Index, Rosenberg Self-Esteem Scale, General Health Questionnaire and Achenbach Child Behaviour Checklist (see Table 1, page 14).

Newpin is another voluntary service that provides intensive support (befriending, therapy and training) to vulnerable parents, mostly mothers, where there is a danger of family breakdown. After an initial home visit, the service is provided in centres. An evaluation commissioned by the Department of Health in the late 1980s (Pound, 1994) reported that mothers attending Newpin had benefited compared to a control group (although the control group was not very well matched), but that sustained involvement of up to 12 months was necessary for the mothers' mental state to improve. A later study of over 200 mothers referred to four Newpin schemes in London was more critical. Fewer than half of those referred to Newpin had gone on to use the service and, of those who had, only half had found that it helped (Oakley et al., 1995).

INTERVENTIONS TO ADDRESS CHILDREN'S MENTAL HEALTH

Coping with children who have emotional and behavioural difficulties is a common reason for families coming into contact with social workers and needing support. Children whose mental health problems are fairly severe may be referred to the child and adolescent mental health (CAMH) service. There are many studies that focus on trials of specific therapies or treatments for specific disorders, but very few that look at the effectiveness of the CAMH service as a whole, in a 'real life' setting, or at the extent to which it alleviates family problems (Barnes-McGuire, Stein and Rosenberg, 1997). Whilst research-based studies often find positive effects, the few studies based on real clinical conditions tend to report little evidence of change (Weisz et al., 1995). An exception was a recent Welsh study investigating long-term outcomes for pre-school children referred to a CAMH service, by comparing 16 referred families who accepted treatment with 10 families who declined the service. Improvements which were still evident two years later were found in child behaviour and maternal mental health in the former group (Hutchings et al., 1998).

There is some evidence of the effectiveness of population-based mental health services and preventive work in communities and schools. A good example is an evaluation in East London of a parent adviser service provided by health visitors and clinical medical officers who were trained and supported by CAMH specialists. The advisers went into the homes of parents whose pre-school children were experiencing multiple psycho-social problems and supported them in managing their children's behaviour. Compared to a control group, the 55 families using the parent adviser service experienced a significant reduction in the severity of their problems, increased parental self-esteem, decreased levels of parental stress and emotional difficulties, more positive constructions of their children, improvements in the home environment, and decreased child behaviour problems (Davis and Spurr, 1998).

Community interventions designed to address the mental health of school-aged children are reviewed in a recent publication in the Barnado's 'What works?' series (Buchanan, 1999). They include problem-solving programmes, anti-bullying programmes, peer support programmes and behaviour support programmes for children at risk of school exclusion. Some evidence is found to support all of these approaches. However, very little of CAMH staff time is currently spent on supporting such community-based work (Audit Commission, 1999).

A controlled trial is currently being undertaken in North Wales of a primary care (community-based) model for CAMH services (Appleton and Hammond-Rowley, 2000). A variety of services is available to all children aged under nine and their families in one small community. They include school-based work on emotional and social competence with whole classes of young children, parenting skills courses at three different levels, and a referral-based family consultation service. Measures taken of all children in the area who attend Nursery, Reception and Year 1 school classes over two years will be compared with the scores of a similar group of children living in a demographically matched community, who receive the usual community services.

SERVICES FOR DISABLED CHILDREN AND THEIR FAMILIES

Rigorous research examining the effectiveness of different services in supporting parents of disabled children is sparse, and the Social Services Inspectorate (SSI) has called for local authorities to do more monitoring of the effectiveness of the services they provide (SSI, 1994, 1998). Most evaluations have been small scale and concentrated on investigating parents' needs and experiences of services, rather than looking at outcomes for parents and children – although parental satisfaction with services is certainly one measure of outcomes. Sloper (1999) reviews research into the kind of services parents value, such as family-based respite care services, parent-to-parent groups, befriending schemes and early intervention programmes like Portage, a home teaching system for pre-school children with special needs. Bryony Beresford and colleagues provide a useful overview of services to support families with a disabled child, and of the characteristics of services which seem to 'work':

> *The evidence so far suggests that a prime characteristic of effective services for a range of needs is the ability to encompass an individual approach to assessing and meeting need, underpinned by respect for the views of family members, openness and honesty in information sharing, and flexibility of provision.* (Beresford et al., 1996, p. 104)

However, relatively few of the studies identified by Beresford or Sloper adopted an experimental design. Of the exceptions, the first was Glendenning's (1986) research into the effects of providing designated key workers ('resource workers') to support families with a disabled child. This study found a number of positive effects for over a hundred families receiving this service, compared with a similarly sized control group. Positive outcomes included higher parental morale, receipt of more practical help, greater satisfaction with respite facilities and less isolation. The greatest value of the service was seen as having someone to talk to, to whom parents could turn for help whenever they needed.

The second study was an evaluation of a parent adviser scheme in East London, using a randomized controlled trial (Davis and Rushton, 1991). This programme has since been extended to support families of non-disabled pre-school children who are under severe stress because of their children's behaviour, as described above. In the original project, families of young children with developmental delay were visited by parent advisers trained in a basic counselling approach. The advisers' role was to explore any issues raised by the parents, including material resources, relationship problems and problems related to the child; to help parents to clarify problems, set goals, formulate plans and carry them out. The results of the study showed that, compared with the control group, mothers seen by the parent advisers rated themselves as better supported by professionals and felt more positive about the child, and the children's developmental progress was greater. Results for the group of socially disadvantaged Bangladeshi mothers were even stronger.

A third study used a quasi-experimental design (with families waiting for the service as a control group) to examine the impact of a family-based respite care scheme on the well-being of mothers of disabled children (Bose, 1991). Although no differences were noted on some of the variables measured, such as the effect on siblings, or numbers of friends and outings, users of the service reported higher levels of social support and morale and lower levels of stress than mothers in the control group.

Early intervention programmes such as Portage have been relatively well evaluated. Research findings suggest that, as with more general early intervention programmes such as Head Start in America, there are positive short-term gains for the child but less clear-cut long-term effects on the child's intellectual development or academic achievement (Cunningham, 1986; Simeonsson et al., 1982). These may not be the only outcome measures to judge the service by; Beresford points out that most parents are very positive about the Portage service and that it increases their sense of competence, which is likely to benefit the child's well-being in the long term (Beresford, 1994; Beresford et al., 1996).

SHORT-TERM FOSTERING

Under the Children Act 1989, short-term accommodation or respite care (brief planned periods away from home with the same carers over several months) can be offered as a family support service to help prevent long-term family breakdown. This service has traditionally been developed to support families with a disabled child, but can also be used for other children who are in need. Research by Aldgate and Bradley (1999) traced the progress over nine months of 60 non-disabled children and families who used short-term fostering, comparing measures taken before and after receiving the service. At the end of the nine months' study period, parents felt better, were more in control of their lives and had reduced their problems, and their expectations of the service had generally been met. As many as 92 per cent of families remained intact. However, there was no comparison group to show whether improvements might have happened anyway.

SOCIAL WORK SUPPORT

The support offered by social workers to children and families is an important aspect of family support, both as a service in itself and as a facilitator and co-ordinator of other services that families may receive. A review by Brian Sheldon of 'social work effectiveness experiments' (Sheldon, 1986) – which covered all kinds of social work, not just that with children and families – concluded that there was some evidence for positive effects under particular circumstances. Social workers were more effective when there was a clearly identified target problem, when a contractual style and a task-centred or behaviourist approach was used, when the work with the client was intensive, and when there was good co-ordination with other agencies.

In a more recent search of over 50 journals, Macdonald, Sheldon and Gillespie (1992) were less optimistic about the evidence for social work effectiveness. They identified 96 studies that evaluated social work practice, either alone or in conjunction with other professionals. Most were US studies, and fewer than one in seven evaluated work with children. Others looked at work with the mentally ill, with juvenile offenders and with older people. Macdonald concludes that there is 'a dearth of empirical data about [this] major area of social work activity' (Macdonald, 1999). One of the problems in attempting to evaluate the effectiveness of support provided by social workers is the difficulty of separating the personal from the professional, since much of what social workers do is through the medium of their personalities and the relationships they establish.

One well-designed study that demonstrated a positive effect of social work support was a large-scale RCT of the Alameda Project (Stein and Gambrill, 1977). This US study aimed to assess whether providing intensive support to parents could improve the chances of their looked-after children returning home. Most of the children were accommodated because of neglect rather than abuse, and parents received structured help from qualified social workers focused on addressing the problems that were preventing rehabilitation. At the end of the study nearly half of the children in the experimental group were returned home or had left foster care, compared to 11 per cent of the controls.

FAMILY GROUP CONFERENCES

Family group conferences (FGCs) are a way of involving families in drawing up plans to ensure the safety of their children. They are not strictly speaking a support service in themselves, but aim to help families identify the support and resources they need to keep their children at home. A study at Portsmouth University (Lupton and Stevens, 1997) compared 20 families who had been through an FGC with 19 families attending traditional child protection conferences. There were a number of methodological difficulties with the study, not least the lack of control over which kinds of cases went to FGCs, and most of the key results concerned process rather than outcomes. Overall, FGC families received *less* direct input and fewer resources from social services departments than those having traditional meetings, but more support from family members and other agencies. Children whose families experienced an FGC were less likely to remain living with their original family. A follow-on study which is currently being undertaken will compare outcomes on a number of tightly defined measures for families allocated randomly to either an FGC or a traditional child protection conference (Lupton and Brown, 1998).

Note

1. Although the term 'parent' is commonly used, in practice most parenting programmes are predominantly attended by mothers.

❸ Measuring outcomes and costs

Many different types of measures have been used in the studies reviewed to collect data on outcomes. They include:

- test scores (e.g. measures of child development, parental mental health, attitudes to parenting)
- interview and survey data (e.g. on children's diet, mothers' reported well-being, housing and employment status)
- observation of children or parent–child interaction (in clinics, homes and schools)
- ratings of user satisfaction with services
- GP and hospital records (e.g. immunization rates, accident and emergency admissions, number of visits to GP surgery)
- changes in legal status (e.g. removal from child protection register, becoming 'looked after').

Table 1 lists some published scales and tests that have been used to assess whether an intervention has led to any change. However, it is important to remember that test scores are only one of the ways in which outcomes may be assessed.

Table 1: A selection of tests and scales used to measure family support outcomes

Measure	Author	Description
Child Development and Behaviour		
Strengths and Difficulties Questionnaire	Goodman (1997)	Measures emotional and behavioural problems in children but with focus on strengths as well as difficulties. 25 statements, e.g. 'often fights with other children or bullies them', rated on 3-point scale. Versions for completion by parents, teachers or older children themselves.
Achenbach Child Behaviour Checklist	Achenbach (1991)	Behaviour rating scale to measure behaviour problems, separate versions for children aged 2–3 and 4–18. Around 100 items, scored by parent/carer on 3-point scale.
Pre-school Behaviour Questionnaire	Behar and Stringfield (1974)	30 descriptions of behaviours commonly found in children aged 3 to 6 (e.g. 'doesn't share toys') which parent/carer rates on 3-point scale.
Child Well-Being Scales	Magura and Moses (1986)	43 items rating extent to which children's needs (physical and psychological, social) are met. Completed by interviewer on basis of home observation, case notes etc.

The Looking After Children Assessment and Action Records	Department of Health (1995)	Detailed materials to assist social workers in assessing how far children's developmental needs are met in 7 areas, including health, education and family relationships.

Parenting

Parenting Stress Index	Abidin (1990)	Assesses sources and levels of stress in parents of young children below secondary-school age. Short form has 36 items rated on 5-point scale, e.g. 'my child makes more demands on me than most children'.
Family Problems Questionnaire	Gibbons (1990)	Also covers parent–child interaction (see below).
Parenting Daily Hassles Scale	Crnic and Greenberg (1990)	Asssesses frequency and impact of 20 potential parenting 'hassles' experienced by adults caring for young children.
Parental Discipline	Arnold et al. (1993)	Measures parenting style and discipline practices in parents of pre-school children. 7-point scale between two alternatives: e.g. 'when my child misbehaves: I do something right away. ... I do something about it later'.
Pleasure in Parenting	Fagot (1995)	Describes 10 typical parent–toddler interactions (e.g. 'putting the child to bed') and asks parents to rate on a 5-point scale from 'dislike' to 'enjoy very much'.
Mellow Parenting Coding System	Mills and Puckering (1992)	Detailed coding system for analysing videotaped observations of parent–child interaction at home. Requires training to use.
Home Observation Measurement of the Environment (HOME Inventory)	Caldwell and Bradley (1984)	Observation schedule for recording aspects of the home environment and parent–child interaction. Separate versions for ages 0–3 and 3–6. Completed by researcher during home visit including interview. Requires training.

Social support and resources

Family Problems Questionnaire	Gibbons (1990)	Developed by researchers at East Anglia University. Contains 39 items introduced as 'a list of problems families often have' which parents score from 'strongly agree' to 'strongly disagree'. Covers social contact, parenting, health, finances and marital problems.
Maternal Social Support Index	Pascoe et al. (1988)	Assesses emotional and practical support provided by a mother's social network. 18 items, self-completion or as part of an interview.
Family Support Scale	Dunst, Trivette and Deal (1988)	Lists 19 potential sources of support (e.g. relatives, parent groups, professional agencies) which are rated on 5-point scale for 'how helpful they have been to you over the past 3–6 months in terms of raising your children'.

Family Resources Scale	Dunst, Trivette and Deal (1988)	Designed to assess how far family has adequate resources (time, money, energy etc.) to meet their needs. Self-completion. 21 items rated from 'not at all' to 'almost always' adequate, e.g. 'food for 2 meals a day', 'time to be with your children'.
Support Functions Scale (short form)	Dunst, Trivette and Deal (1988)	Lists 12 different types of assistance (e.g. 'someone to talk to about things that worry you', 'someone to do things with your child'), rated by respondent on a 5-point scale for how much they need help in these areas.

Adult mental health/emotional well-being

General Health Questionnaire (GHQ)	Goldberg (1992)	The most commonly used measure of distress and mental health. Assesses present state in relation to usual, e.g. 'have you recently lost much sleep over worry?', on 4-point scale. Available in various forms, e.g. GHQ12, GHQ28, GHQ30, GHQ60.
Rosenberg Self-Esteem Scale	Rosenberg (1965)	Widely used measure of self-esteem. Respondents are asked to agree or disagree on a 4-point scale with 10 statements such as 'at times I think I am no good at all'.
Rutter Malaise Inventory	Rutter, Tizard and Whitmore (1970)	Short measure with simple yes/no response to 24 questions, e.g. 'Are you easily upset or irritated?'
Beck Depression Inventory	Beck, Steer and Garbin (1988)	Specific focus on depression (1 element of GHQ). 21 items reated on 4-point scale, e.g. 'I feel I have nothing to look forward to'. Short form also available.

Satisfaction with services

Measure of Processes of Care (MPOC)	King, Rosenbaum and King (1997)	Measures delivery of services rather than outcomes for individuals. 56-item questionnaire on quality of services received, designed for completion by parents of disabled children but could be adapted for other services.

Most of these measures attempt to show whether a service has had an impact on a particular child or family. However, the effectiveness of family support services can also be assessed at the community level. This is one of the approaches adopted in the guidance for the 'trailblazer' areas setting up locally based schemes to support parents with young children under the government's Sure Start programme (Sure Start Unit, 1999). Local programmes are expected to assess the impact of their services through compiling initial baseline data on indicators such as the percentage of children with avoidable speech delay at 18 months and three years, breast-feeding rates at birth and six weeks, and the number of children excluded from primary schools.

APPROPRIATE MEASURES   Whether outcomes are assessed at an individual or community level, a key issue is that the outcome measures selected need to be appropriate to the aims and objectives of the service that is being evaluated. 'The heart of service evaluation is the setting of appropriate standards against which to measure performance' (Logan, 1999). Although standardized scales are generally seen as preferable, it is probably better to use a measuring tool that is 'fit for its purpose' (measures what the intervention aims to achieve) rather than one which – although valid and reliable – is less well matched to what the service could expect to achieve, especially in the short term. McCroskey and Meezan (1998) have pointed out that many evaluations emphasize child development outcomes because there are a number of well-established measures in this field, even though most family support services are aimed at adult family members.

It is also important to take account of what the users of services would see as desirable outcomes. The measures chosen by researchers may not necessarily be those which are most important to children and families, and consulting with users in advance of an evaluation may help to ensure that appropriate outcomes are being assessed (Edwards, Oakley and Popay, 1999; McAuley, 1999). Otherwise, 'the measurement of irrelevant objectives may result in services being congratulated for being very efficient at doing completely the wrong things' (Beresford et al., 1996, p. 16).

A third consideration when choosing appropriate measures is the timescale over which any impact is likely to occur. Most of the studies reviewed here consider outcomes over a relatively short time span. Where children have been followed over many years, as in the Perry/High Scope project, other outcome measures may be possible. For example, at age 19 the children who had taken part in the High Scope programme were less likely to have needed special educational support or to have become pregnant; they were more likely to have completed schooling and to have a job (Berrueta-Clement et al., 1984). At age 27, they had a higher income level and rate of home ownership and were less likely to have needed to use social services in the last ten years or to have been arrested for drug offences (Schweinhart, Barnes and Weikart, 1993).

However, such long-term studies are costly, and few and far between. Funding for research usually only allows the effectiveness of interventions to be considered over a relatively short period: sometimes six months and rarely more than two years. This will obviously affect the kind of impact an intervention can be expected to produce, and the outcome measures that can be used.

COST EFFECTIVENESS

Very few studies of family support services include information about the costs of interventions or compare the benefits of different types of service in relation to their costs (this is known as a 'cost effectiveness' or 'cost benefit' analysis).[1] Many local authorities have little information about unit costs of services they provide or commission to support families, although an audit of services for children in need carried out by all English social services departments in February 2000 should help to remedy this situation (Children in Need Project Group, 1999).

A handful of the studies reviewed in this paper do provide information on cost effectiveness, although it is often unclear how costs have been calculated. Cunningham, Bremner and Boyle (1995) compared community-based and individual parent training programmes for families of pre-school children with disruptive behaviour disorders. The group programmes in the community were not only more effective but also six times as cost effective, with a group size of 18. In England, Sutton (1992) compared three different methods of training parents to manage difficult children: group, home visiting and telephone; and found all three led to improvements compared to a waiting-list control group. Although a cost benefit analysis was not carried out, Sutton claims that 'parents can be as effectively trained by means of regular telephone calls as by the procedures which are more expensive of trainer time'. However, there was a greater falling-away of benefits at one year follow-up among the telephone method group, and also it was not considered appropriate for parents whose children had more serious behaviour disorders.

The most widely quoted example of a cost benefit analysis concerns the High Scope/Perry Preschool programme. It has been calculated that for every dollar spent on providing the service, 7 dollars are later gained due to reduced spending on special education and welfare benefits, and to higher earnings and less crime (Schweinhart, Barnes and Weikart, 1993). The saving to the public purse is only part of this, some 2.5 dollars (Holtermann, 1998), but this study has been very influential in supporting the case for increased expenditure on early years' services for disadvantaged families.

The preliminary evaluation of eight EECs (Bertram and Pascal, 1999) has made similar claims that for every £1 spent on family support, £8 is saved on alternative services. This is based not on the basis of long-term outcomes compared to a control group, but by calculating the cost of alternative services that might have been needed had certain families not been supported by the centre, such as foster care and rehabilitation programmes. However, without a comparison group of families in similar circumstances but not attending an EEC, it is impossible to know whether these services would have been provided, or whether the families would have improved anyway.

There is increasing interest in funding studies of both costs and outcomes of services for children in need. The Department of Health, under a new research initiative called 'Costs and Outcomes of Services to Children in Need', has commissioned a series of research projects beginning in late 1999/early 2000, to investigate the costs and outcomes of services such as children's homes, foster care, non-infant adoptions, adolescent support teams and different interventions for sexually abused children. In Wales, the Wales Office of Research and Development for Health and Social Care has funded an investigation into the feasibility of using community level indicators to demonstrate the impact of family support services (Denniston et al., 1999), and is supporting an ongoing study comparing costs and outcomes of family support services for children in need in two authorities in North Wales (see note to page vii).

Note

1. A good description of the different techniques used in economic analysis such as cost effectiveness analysis, cost benefit analysis and option appraisal, and the ways in which they can be applied to social welfare programmes, is provided by Holtermann (1998).

4 Conclusions

From this overview of the available research, a number of tentative conclusions may be drawn about the types of services which are effective in supporting families who are experiencing difficulties in their lives. There is good evidence for the effectiveness of high quality early education and day care services in improving the life chances of children from disadvantaged families, and for some parenting programmes – especially those that are group based and help parents to develop effective praise and reinforcement techniques. There is much anecdotal evidence for the effectiveness of family centres, but little hard evidence – especially for open access centres where evaluation poses particular difficulties.

Support provided by trained home visitors has been shown to improve mothers' well-being and to have positive effects on mother–child interaction, although most of the research has been conducted in the USA. Evidence for UK schemes such as Home-Start is suggestive but studies with a control group have not yet been carried out. There is some evidence for the effectiveness of population-based mental health services and preventive work in communities and schools in reducing child behaviour problems, and of the positive impact of services to support the parents of disabled children, including a 'key worker' system to provide one point of access for families to services provided by different agencies. A key aspect of many successful family support services appears to be the way in which they are delivered, particularly the nature of the relationship between provider and user.

One aspect that has not been addressed in many of the studies is the extent to which they are accessible to and used by the families who need them. Given that family support services are usually used on a voluntary basis, they need to be attractive to parents and children (Statham, 1994). Yet Oakley, Rajan and Turner (1998) found that nearly half of the families referred to Home-Start and nearly two-thirds of those referred to Newpin either did not use the service or did so only briefly. Drop-out from parenting programmes can also be high, but information is not always included on this – or, where it is, it is not explained.

Much of the evidence for the effectiveness of family support services comes from the USA, where there is a strong tradition of systematic programme evaluation and a particular approach to family support. The findings from this research need to be applied with caution in different social welfare contexts, and it needs to be recognized that different policies and ways of thinking about children would lead to different ways of conceptualizing the evaluation of family support.

In the UK, there is a valuable tradition of research into how family support services are set up and delivered, and what users think of them (although the views of children themselves are often neglected). There has been little information to date on the costs of providing family support services, although this is beginning to be addressed; and hardly any cost benefit analyses comparing the costs of different types of support services, or of providing a service compared to doing nothing at all. There is a need for more well-designed studies of the effectiveness of UK family support services using a range of methods, not only controlled trials but also in-depth studies to explore the characteristics of effective services from the perspective of different individuals within the family as well as of professionals in different agencies. Further work is also needed to develop appropriate outcome measures for family support services, taking account of the views of service users.

⑤ References

Abidin, R. (1990), *Parenting Stress Index*. Odessa, FL: Psychological Assessment Resources Inc.

Achenbach, T. (1991), *Manual for the Child Behaviour Checklist*. Burlington, VT: University of Vermont.

Aldgate, J. and Bradley, M. (1999), *Supporting families through short-term fostering*. London: The Stationery Office.

Appleton, P. and Hammond-Rowley, S. (2000), 'Addressing the population burden of child and adolescent mental health problems: a primary care model'. *Child Psychology and Psychiatry Review*, 5, 1, 9–16.

Arnold, D., O'Leary, S., Wolff, L. and Acker, M. (1993), 'The parenting scale: a measure of dysfunctional parenting in discipline situations'. *Psychological Assessment*, 5, 2, 137–144.

Audit Commission (1994), *Seen but not heard*. London: HMSO.

— (1999), *Children in mind: child and adolescent mental health services*. London: Audit Commission.

Barlow, J. (1997), *Systematic review of the effectiveness of parent-training programmes in improving behaviour problems in children aged 3–10 years*. Oxford: Health Services Research Unit, Department of Public Health.

Barnes-McGuire, J., Stein, A. and Rosenberg, W. (1997), 'Evidence-based medicine and child mental health services: a broad approach to evaluation is needed'. *Children and Society*, 11, 88–96.

Beck, A., Steer, R. and Garbin, M. (1988), 'Psychometric properties of the Beck Depression Inventory: twenty-five years of evaluation'. *Clinical Psychology Review*, 8, 1, 77–100.

Behar, L. and Stringfield, S. (1974), 'A behaviour rating scale for the preschool child'. *Developmental Psychology*, 10, 601–610.

Beresford, B. (1994), *Positively parents: caring for a disabled child*. London: HMSO.

Beresford, B., Sloper, P., Baldwin, S. and Newman, T. (1996) *What works in services for families with a disabled child?* Barkingside, Essex: Barnado's.

Berrueta-Clement, J.R., Schweinhart, L.J., Barnett, W.S., Epstein, A.S. and Weikart, D.P. (1984), *Changed lives: the effects of the Perry Preschool Program on youths through age 19*. Michigan: High/Scope Press.

Bertram, T. and Pascal, C. (2000), *Early Excellence Centres: first findings*. London: DfEE.

Bose, R. (1991), 'The effect of a family support scheme on maternal mental health of mothers caring for children with mental handicaps'. *Research, Policy and Planning*, 9, 2–8.

Buchanan, A. (1999), *What works in family support? Responding to children and young people with emotional and behavioural problems*. Barkingside, Essex: Barnado's.

Caldwell, B. and Bradley, M. (1984), *Home observation for measurement of the environment – administration manual* (revised edition). Arkansas: University of Arkansas.

Cameron, C. and Statham, J. (1997), 'Sponsored places: the use of independent day care services to support children in need'. *British Journal of Social Work*, 27, 85–100.

Cannan, C. and Warren, C. (eds) (1997), *Social action with children and families: a community development approach to child and family welfare.* London: Routledge.

Cheetham, J., Fuller, R., McIvor, G. and Petch, A. (1997), *Evaluating social work effectiveness.* Milton Keynes: Open University Press.

Children in Need Project Group (1999), *The Children in Need pilot: results and feedback to participating authorities.* Unpublished paper, see www.doh.gov.uk/cin/cin.htm

Children in Wales (1998), *The healthy child: resource materials for parent groups.* Cardiff: Children in Wales.

Crnic, K.A. and Greenberg (1990), 'Minor parenting stresses with young children'. *Child Development*, 61, 1628–1637.

Cunningham, C. (1986), 'Early intervention: some findings from the Manchester cohort of children with Down's syndrome'. In M. Bishop, M. Copley and J. Porter (eds), *Portage: more than a teaching programme?* Windsor: NFER-Nelson.

Cunningham, C., Bremner, R. and Boyle, M. (1995), 'Large group community-based parenting programs for families of preschoolers at risk for disruptive behaviour disorders: utilization, cost effectiveness, and outcome'. *Journal of Child Psychology and Psychiatry*, 36, 7, 1141–1159.

Davey, D., Holland, S. and Pithouse, A. (1999), *Newport Family Centre: a case study evaluation 1996–1999.* Unpublished final report, School of Social Sciences, University of Wales Cardiff.

Davis, H. and Rushton, R. (1991) 'Counselling and supporting parents of children with developmental delay: a research evaluation'. *Journal of Mental Deficiency Research*, 35, 89–112.

Davis, H. and Spurr, P. (1998), 'Parent counselling: an evaluation of a community child mental health service'. *Journal of Child Psychology and Psychiatry*, 39, 3, 365–376.

Denniston, K., Pithouse, A., Bloor, M. and O'Leary, M. (1999), *Developing a model of economic analysis in family support services: the case of a neighbourhood family centre in Blaenau Gwent.* Unpublished report, School of Social Sciences, University of Wales Cardiff.

Department of Health (1995), *Child protection: messages from research.* London: HMSO.

— (forthcoming), *The Children Act now: messages from research.* London: The Stationery Office.

Dunst, C., Trivette, C. and Deal, A. (1988), *Enabling and empowering families: principles and guidelines for practice.* Cambridge, MA: Brookline Books.

— (1994), *Supporting and strengthening families. Vol 1: methods, strategies and practice.* Cambridge, MA: Brookline Books.

Edwards, J., Oakley, A. and Popay, J. (1999), 'Service users' and providers' perspectives on welfare needs'. In F. Williams, J. Popay and A. Oakley. *Welfare research: a critical review.* London: UCL Press.

Fagot, B. (1995), Development of a pleasure in parenting scale'. *Early Development and Parenting*, 4, 2, 75–82.

Frost, N., Johnson, L., Stein, M. and Wallis, L. (1996), *Negotiated friendship: Home-Start and the delivery of family support.* Leicester: Home-Start UK.

Ghate, D., Shaw, C. and Hazel, N. (2000), *Fathers and family centres: engaging fathers in preventive services.* York: Joseph Rowntree Foundation.

Gibbons, J. (1990), *Family support and prevention: studies in local areas.* London: HMSO.

— (1991), 'Children in need and their families: outcomes of referrals to social services'. *British Journal of Social Work*, 21, 217–227.

Gibbons, J. (ed.) (1992), *The Children Act 1989 and family support: principles into practice.* London: HMSO.

Glendenning, C. (1986), *A single door: social work with families of disabled children.* London: Allen and Unwin.

Goldberg, D. (1992), *General Health Questionnaire (GHQ-12).* Windsor: NFER-Nelson.

Goodman, R. (1997), 'The Strengths and Difficulties Questionnaire: a research note'. *Journal of Child Psychology and Psychiatry*, 38, 5, 581–586.

Guralnick, M. (ed.) (1997), *The effectiveness of early intervention*. Baltimore, MD: Paul Brookes Publishing.

Hardiker, P., Exton, K. and Barker, M. (1995), *The prevention of child abuse: a framework for analysing services*. London: National Commission of Inquiry into the Prevention of Child Abuse.

Hearn, B. (1995), *Child and family support and protection: a practical approach*. London: National Children's Bureau.

Higgins, K., Pinkerton, J. and Devine, P. (1997), *Family support in Northern Ireland: perspectives from practice*. Belfast: Centre for Child Care Research.

Hill, M., Triseliotis, J., Borland, M. and Lambert, L. (1995), 'Outcomes of social work intervention with young people'. In M. Hill and J. Aldgate (eds) (1996), *Child welfare services: developments in law policy, practice, research*. London: Jessica Kingsley.

Holtermann, S. (1995), *All our futures: the impact of public expenditure and fiscal policies on Britain's children and young people*. Barkingside, Essex: Barnado's.

Holtermann, S. (1998), *Weighing it up: applying economic evaluations to social welfare programmes*. York: Joseph Rowntree Foundation.

Hutchings, J., Nash, S., Smith, M. and Parry, G. (1998) Long-term outcome for pre-school children referred to a CAMH team for behaviour management problems. Bangor: School of Psychology, University of Wales Bangor.

Jack, G. (1997), 'An ecological approach to social work with children and families'. *Child and Family Social Work*, 2, 109–120.

Johnson, Z. and Molloy, B. (1995), 'The community mothers programme – empowerment of parents by parents'. *Children and Society*, 9, 2, 73–83.

King, G., Rosenbaum, P. and King. S. (1997), 'Evaluating a family-centred service using a measure of parents' perceptions'. *Child: Care, Health and Development*, 23, 47–62.

Knapp, M. (1984), *The economics of social care*. London: Macmillan.

Laurent, C. (2000), The real life class. *The Guardian*, 11 April 2000.

Lawes, G. (1992), 'Individual parent training implemented by nursery nurses: evaluation of a programme for mothers of pre-school children'. *Behavioural Psychotherapy*, 20, 239–256.

Leach, P. and Barnes, J. (2000), *Families, children and child care: a prospective study of various kinds of care on children's development from birth to five*. Paper presented at Parent–Child 2000 conference, London, 13 April 2000.

Lloyd, E. (1997), 'The role of the family centre in family support'. In C. Cannan and C. Warren (eds), *Social action with children and families: a community development approach to child and family welfare*. London: Routledge.

Lloyd, E. (ed.) (1999), *Parenting matters: what works in parenting education?* Barkingside, Essex: Barnado's.

Logan, S. (1999), 'Evaluating services for children with disabilities and their families'. *Child: Care, Health and Development*, 25, 2, 81–83.

Lupton, C. and Brown, L. (1998), *Do family group conferences produce better outcomes for children than traditional child protection conferences?* Proposal for project grant to Nuffield Institute and the Centre for Evidence-based Social Services.

Lupton, C. and Stevens, M. (1997), *Family outcomes: following through on family group conferences*. Portsmouth: Portsmouth University, Social Services Research and Information Unit.

McAuley, C. (1999), *The family support outcomes study*. Belfast: Queen's University.

McCroskey, J. and Meezan, W. (1998), 'Family-centred services: approaches and effectiveness'. *Protecting Children from Abuse and Neglect*, 8, 1, 54–71.

Macdonald, G., Sheldon, B. and Gillespie, J. (1992), 'Contemporary studies of the effectiveness of social work'. *British Journal of Social Work*, 22, 615–642.

Macdonald, G. (1996), 'Ice therapy: why we need randomised controlled trials'. In P. Alderson et al., *What works? Effective social interventions in child welfare*. Barkingside, Essex: Barnado's.

Macdonald, G. (1999), *Social work and its evaluation: a methodological dilemma?* In F. Williams, J. Popay and A. Oakley, *Welfare research: a critical review*. London: UCL Press.

McKey, H., Condelli, L., Ganson, H., Barrett, B., McConkey, C. and Plantz, M. (1985), *The impact of Head Start on children, families and communities*. Washington DC: The Head Start Bureau.

Magura, S. and Moses, B. (1986), *Outcome measures for child welfare services: theory and applications*. Washington DC: Child Welfare League of America.

Mills, M. and Puckering, C. (1992), *The Mellow Parenting training manual*. London: Department of Child and Adolescent Psychiatry, Bloomfield Centre, Guy's Hospital.

Mooney, A. and Munton, A. (1997), *Research and policy in early childhood services: time for a new agenda*. London: Institute of Education.

Newman, T. and Roberts, H. (1999), 'Assessing effectiveness'. In E. Lloyd (ed.), *Parenting matters: what works in parenting education?* Barkingside, Essex: Barnado's.

Oakley, A. (1996), 'Who's afraid of the randomised controlled trial? The challenge of evaluating the potential of social interventions'. In P. Alderson et al., *What works? Effective social interventions in child welfare*. Barkingside, Essex: Barnado's.

Oakley, A., Mauthner, M., Rajan, L. and Turner, H. (1995), 'Supporting vulnerable families: an evaluation of Newpin'. *Health Visitor*, 68, 5, 188–191.

Oakley, A., Rajan, L. and Grant, A. (1990), 'Social support and pregnancy outcome'. *British Journal of Obstetrics and Gynaecology*, 97, 155–162.

Oakley, A., Rajan, L. and Turner, H. (1998), 'Evaluating parent support initiatives: lessons from two case studies'. *Health and Social Care in the Community*, 6, 5, 318–330.

Oakley, A., Rigby, D., Rajan, L. and Hickey, D. (1996), 'Social support in pregnancy: does it have long term effects?' *Journal of Reproductive and Infant Psychology*, 14, 7, 22.

Olds, D., Eckenrode, J., Henderson, C. et al. (1997), 'Long term effects of home visitation on maternal life course and child abuse and neglect: fifteen year follow-up of a randomized trial'. *Journal of the American Medical Association*, 278, 637–643.

Oliver, C., Smith, M. and Barker, S. (1997), *Effectiveness of early interventions*. London: Thomas Coram Research Unit, Institute of Education.

Parker, R. (1991), 'Principles of measurement and evaluation'. In R. Parker (ed.), *Looking after children: assessing outcomes in child care*. London: HMSO.

Parton, N. (1999), *Some thoughts on the relationship between theory and practice in social work*. Paper presented at ESRC-funded seminar series on theorizing social work, 26 May 1999.

Pascoe, J., Ialonge, N., Hom, W. and Reinhardt, M. (1988), 'The reliability and validity of the Maternal Social Support Index'. *Family Medicine*, 20, 4, 271–275.

Piachaud, D. and Sutherland, H. (2000), *How effective is the British government's attempt to reduce poverty?* CASEpaper 38. London: London School of Economics.

Pithouse, A. and Lindsell, S. (1996), 'Child protection services: comparison of a referred family centre and a field social work service in South Wales'. *Research on Social Work Practice*, 6, 4, 473–491.

Pithouse, A. and Holland, S. (1999), 'Open access family centres and their users: positive results, some doubts and new departures'. *Children and Society*, 13, 167–178.

Pound, A. (1994), *NEWPIN: a befriending and therapeutic network for carers of young children*. London: HMSO/National Newpin.

Puckering, C., Mills, M., Cox, A., Maddox, H., Evans, J. and Rogers, J. (1999), *Improving the quality of family support: an intensive parenting programme: Mellow Parenting*. Draft Final Report to the Department of Health.

Roberts, I. (1996), 'Family support and the health of children'. *Children and Society*, 10, 3, 217–224.

Roberts, S. and Statham, J. (1999), *Positive parents: evaluating the use of the healthy child materials in two family centres*. Cardiff: Children in Wales.

Rosenberg, M. (1965), *Society and the adolescent self image*. Princeton, NJ: Princeton University Press.

Rutter, M., Tizard, J. and Whitmore, K. (1970), *Education, health and behaviour*. London: Longman.

Schweinhart, L.J., Barnes, H.V. and Weikart, D.P. (1993), *The High/Scope preschool study through age 27*. Ypsilanti, MI: High/Scope Educational Foundation.

Sheldon, B. (1986), 'Social work effectiveness experiments: review and implications'. *British Journal of Social Work*, 16, 223–242.

Shinman, S. (1994), *Family album: snapshots of Home-Start in words and pictures*. Leicester: Home-Start UK.

Simeonsson, R.J., Cooper, D.M. and Scheiner, A.P. (1982), 'A review and analysis of the effectiveness of early intervention programmes'. *Pediatrics*, 69, 635–641.

Sloper, P. (1999), 'Models of service support for parents of disabled children. What do we know? What do we need to know?' *Child: Care, Health and Development*, 25, 2, 85–99.

Smith, C. (1997), *Developing parenting programmes*. London: National Children's Bureau.

Smith, T. (1996), *Family centres and bringing up young children*. London: HMSO.

— (1999), 'Neighbourhood and preventive strategies with children and families: what works?' *Children and Society*, 13, 265–277.

Social Services Inspectorate (1994), *Services to disabled children and their families*. London: HMSO.

— (1998), *Inspection of services to disabled children and their families*. London: The Stationery Office.

Statham, J. (1994), *Childcare in the community: the provision of open access services for young children in family centres*. London: Save the Children.

Statham, J., Dillon, J. and Moss, P. (2000), 'Sponsored day care in a changing world'. *Children and Society*, 14, 23–36.

Stein, T. and Gambrill, E. (1977), 'Facilitating decision making in foster care'. *Social Services Review*, 51, 502–521.

Stevens, M. (1999), 'Assessing outcomes in child welfare: a critical review'. *Research Policy and Planning*, 17, 1, 26–32.

Sure Start Unit (1999) *Sure Start: a guide for trailblazers*. London: DfEE.

Sutton, C. (1992), 'Training parents to manage difficult children: a comparison of methods'. *Behavioural Psychotherapy*, 20, 115–139.

Sylva, K., Siraj-Blatchford, I. et al. (1999), *Characteristics of pre-school environments: a longitudinal study funded by the DfEE 1997–2003*. Technical paper 6. London: Institute of Education.

Trinder, L. (1996), 'Social work research: the state of the art (or science)'. *Child and Family Social Work*, 1, 233–242.

Van der Eyken, W. (1982). *Home-Start: a four year evaluation*. Leicester: Home-Start UK.

Webster-Stratton, C., Kolpacoff, M. and Hollingsworth, T. (1988), 'Self-administered videotape therapy for families with conduct-problem children: comparison with two cost-effective treatments and a control group'. *Journal of Consulting and Clinical Psychology*, 56, 4, 558–566.

Weisz, J., Donenberg, G., Han, S. and Kauneckis, D. (1995), 'Child and adolescent psychotherapy outcomes in experiments versus clinics: why the disparity?' *Journal of Abnormal Child Psychology*, 23, 1, 83–106.

Williams, F., Popay, J. and Oakley, A. (1999), *Welfare research: a critical review*. London: UCL Press.

Zoritch, B. and Roberts, I. (1997), 'The health and welfare effects of day care for pre-school children: a systematic review of randomised controlled trials'. In Cochrane Database of Systematic Reviews, last updated September 1997.